The Three Little Pigs

Les Trois Petits Cochons

MOOLI PRINT
Bilingual Books

First published 2023 by Mooliprint

978-1-915963-98-7

© 2023 Mooliprint

All rights reserved.

Without limiting the rights under copyright reserved above, no part of this publication may be reproduced, stored in a retrieval system, or transmitted in any form or by any means, electronic, mechanical, photocopying, recording or otherwise, without the prior permission of the publisher.

Once upon a time, there were three little pigs.

Il était une fois, il y avait trois petits cochons.

They left to build their own homes.

Ils sont partis pour construire leurs propres maisons.

The first pig built his house out of straw.

Le premier cochon construisit sa maison en paille.

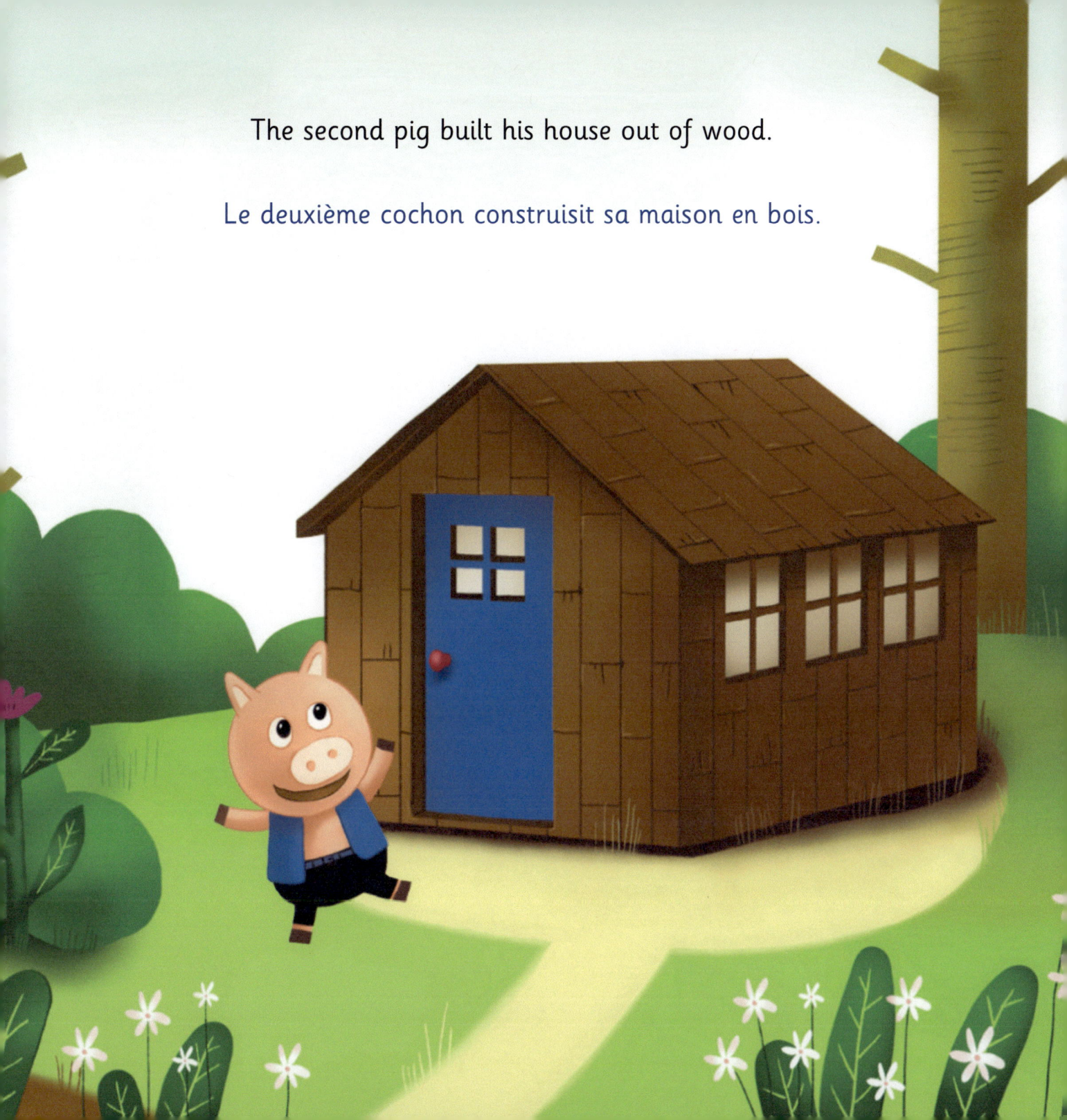

The second pig built his house out of wood.

Le deuxième cochon construisit sa maison en bois.

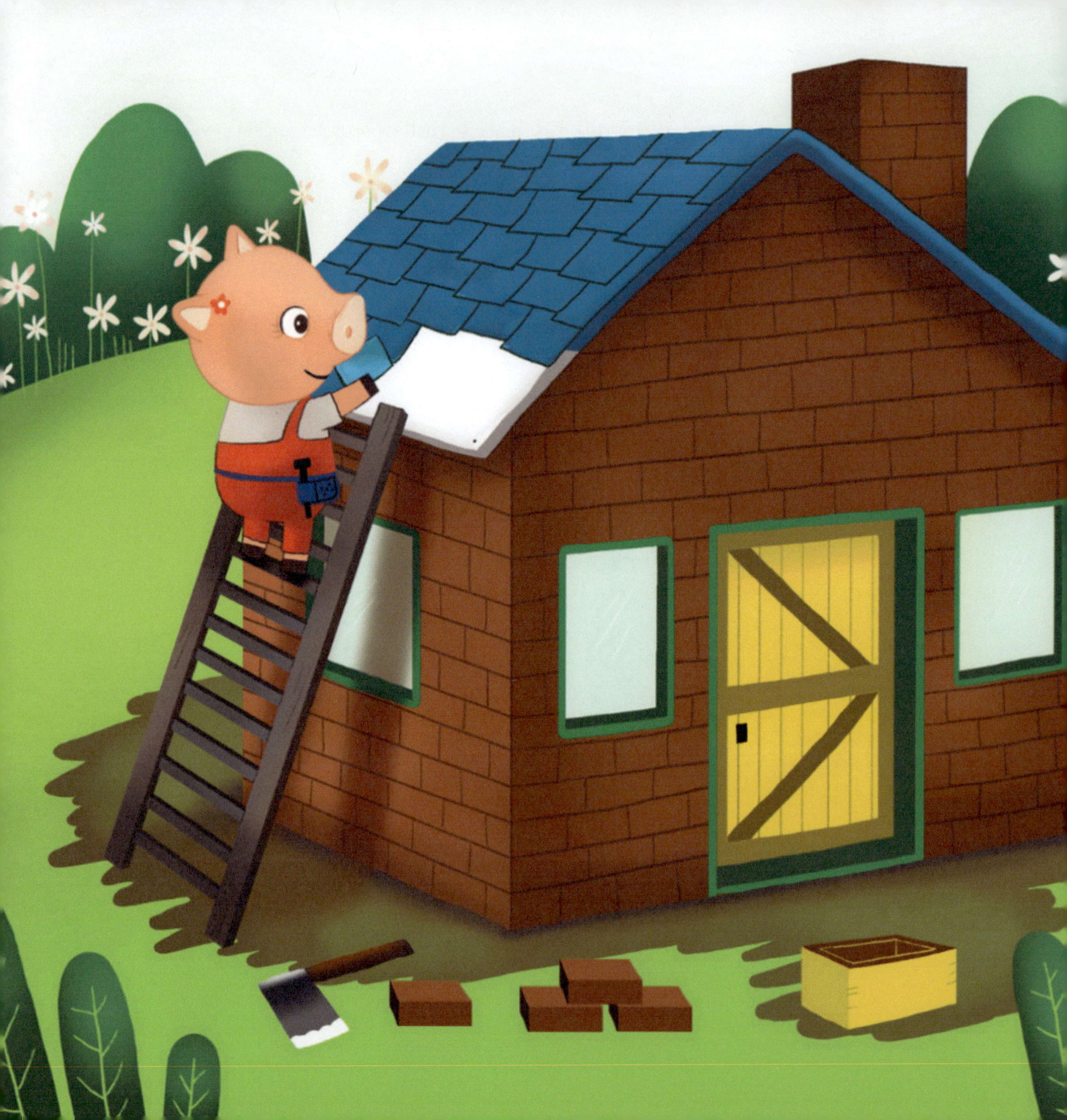

The third pig built her house out of bricks.

La troisième cochonne construisit sa maison en briques.

They were pleased with their work,

Ils étaient satisfaits de leur travail,

but they were unaware of a big, bad wolf nearby.

mais ils ne savaient pas qu'il y avait un grand méchant loup tout près.

The next morning, the big bad wolf came across the first house.

Le lendemain matin, le grand méchant loup tomba sur la première maison.

"Little pig, little pig, let me come in," said the wolf.

« Petit cochon, petit cochon, laisse-moi entrer », dit le loup.

"No, no, no! I won't let you in!" said the little pig.

« Non, non, non ! Je ne te laisserai pas entrer ! » dit le petit cochon.

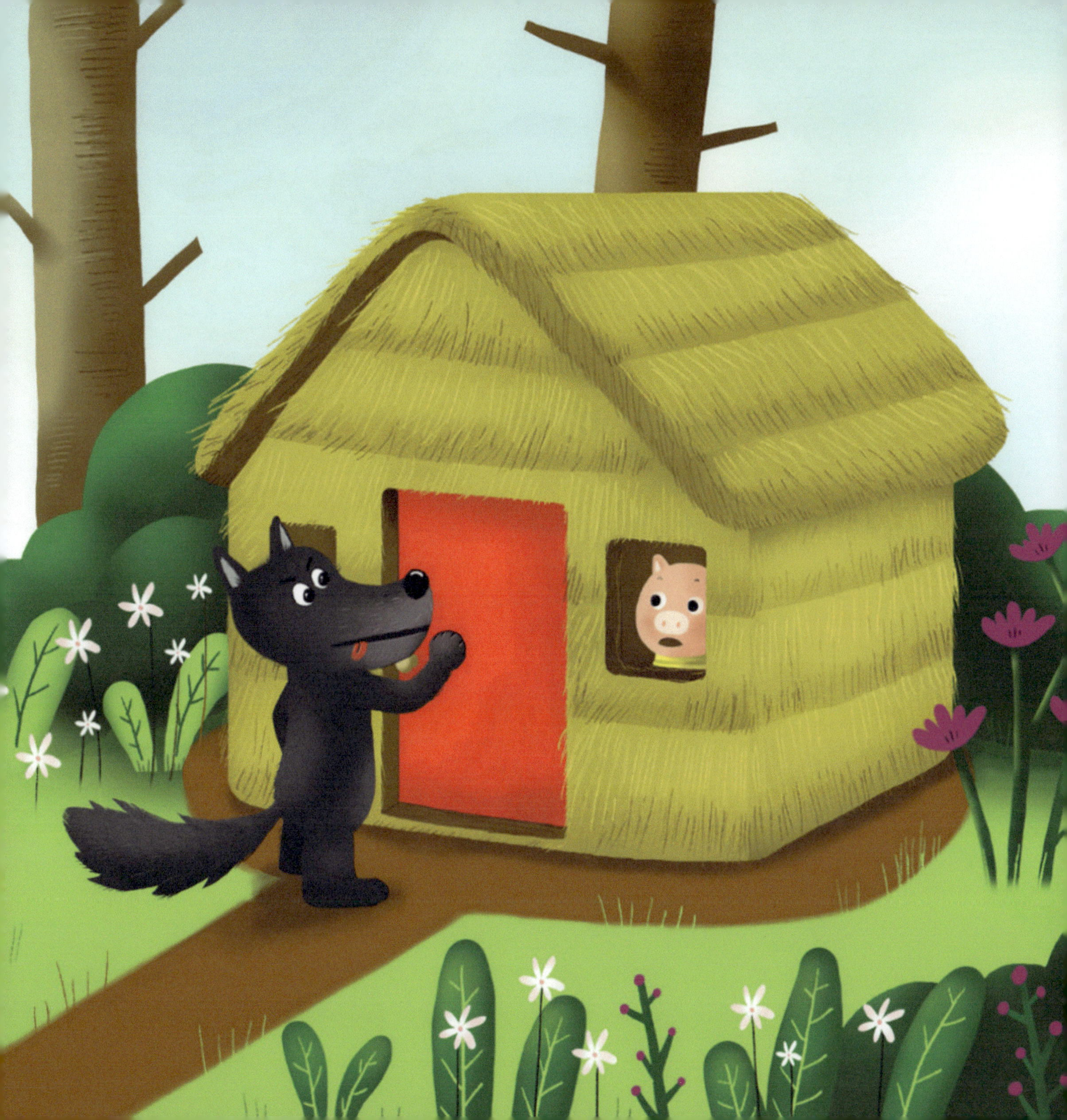

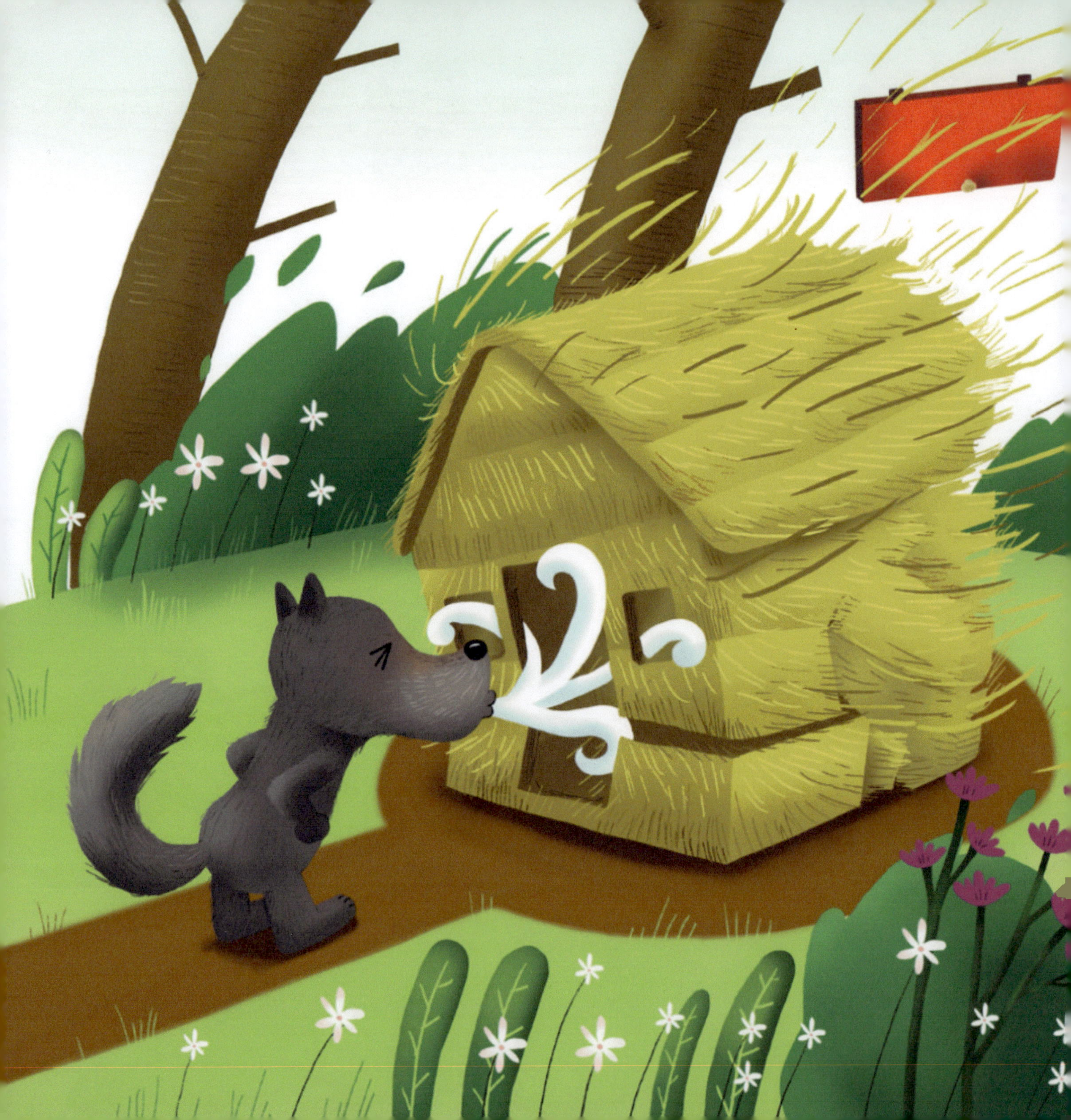

"Then I'll huff and I'll puff and I'll blow your house down!" said the wolf.

« Alors je vais souffler, je vais souffler et je vais faire sauter ta maison ! » dit le loup.

He blew and blew and blew the house down!

Il souffla, souffla et fit s'effondrer la maison !

The little pig escaped.

Le petit cochon s'échappa.

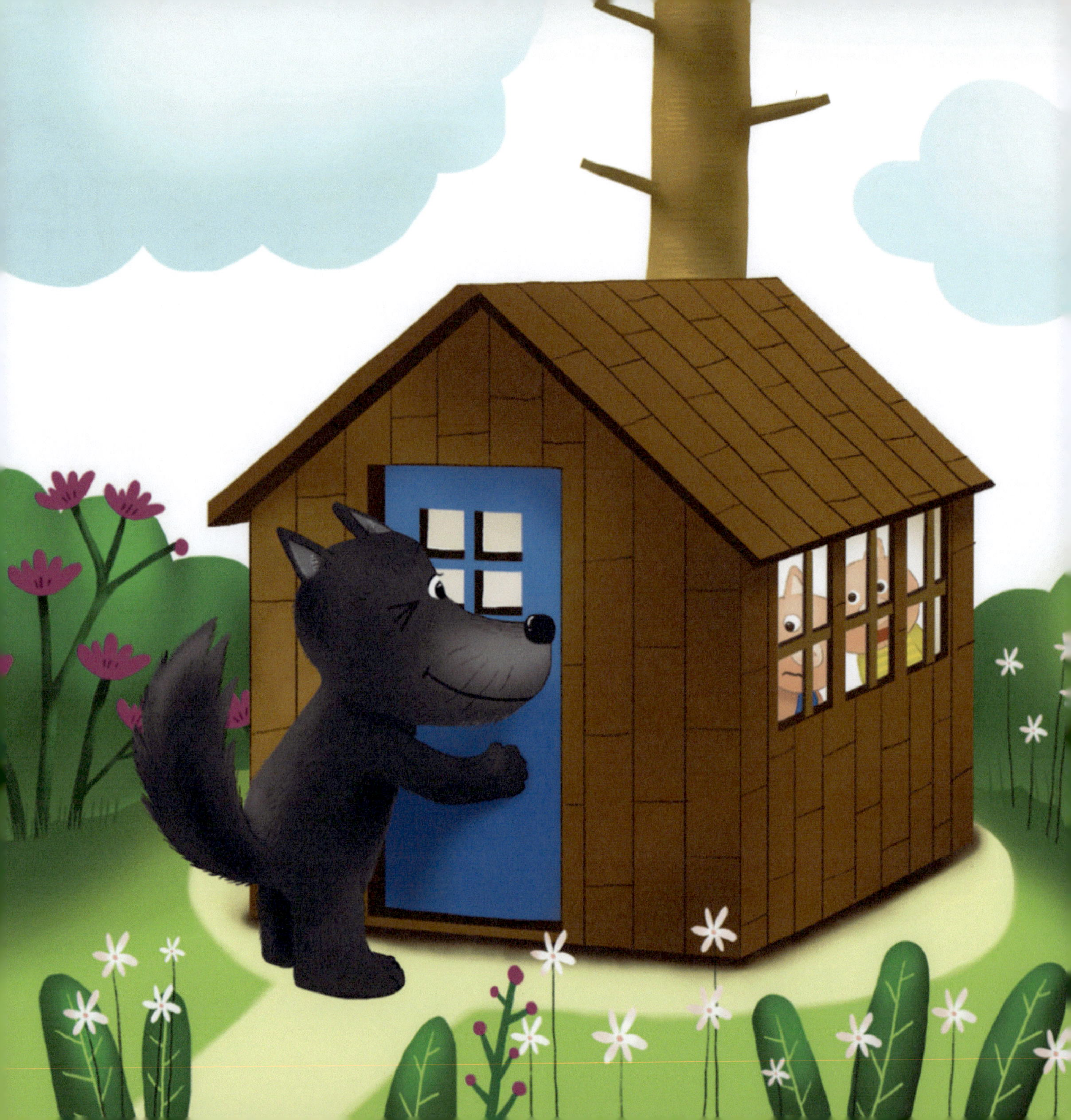

The next day, the wolf returned and knocked on the blue door.

Le lendemain, le loup vint frapper à la porte bleue.

"Little pigs, little pigs, let me come in," said the wolf.

« Petits cochons, petits cochons, laissez-moi entrer », dit le loup.

"No, no, no! We won't let you in!" said the little pigs.

« Non, non, non ! Nous ne te laisserons pas entrer ! » dirent les petits cochons.

"Then I'll huff and I'll puff and I'll blow your house down!" said the wolf.

« Alors je vais souffler, je vais souffler et je vais faire sauter votre maison ! » dit le loup.

He blew and blew and blew the house down!

Il souffla, souffla et fit s'effondrer la maison !

The little pigs ran to their sister's house made of bricks.

Les petits cochons coururent jusqu'à la maison en briques de leur sœur.

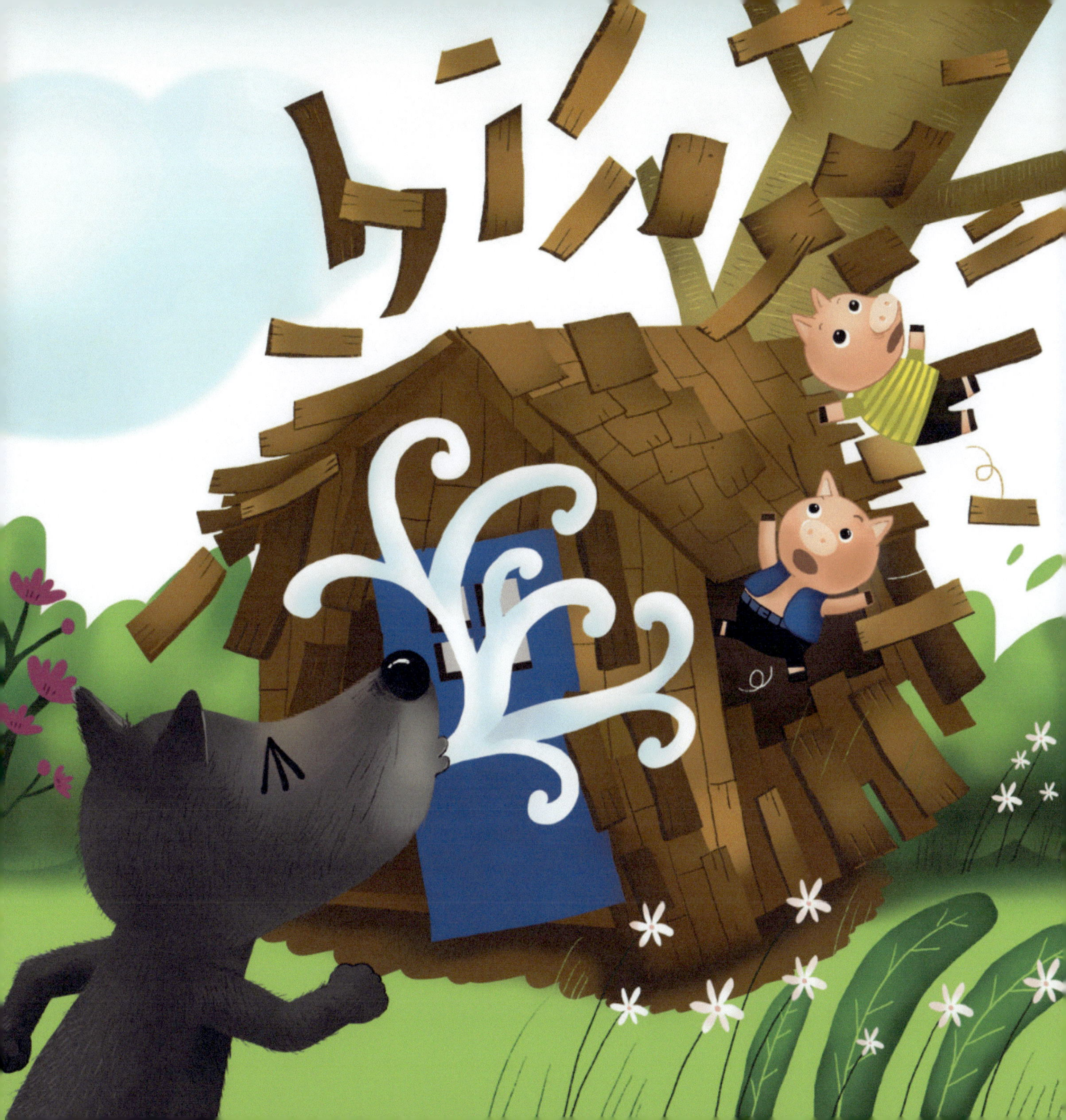

"Little pigs, little pigs, let me in," said the wolf.

« Petits cochons, petits cochons, laissez-moi entrer », dit le loup.

"No, no, no! We won't let you in!" said the little pigs.

« Non, non, non ! Nous ne te laisserons pas entrer », dirent les petits cochons.

"Then I'll huff and I'll puff and I'll blow your house down!" said the wolf, and he blew and he blew and blew!

« Alors je vais souffler, souffler et faire exploser votre maison ! » dit le loup, et il souffla, souffla et souffla !

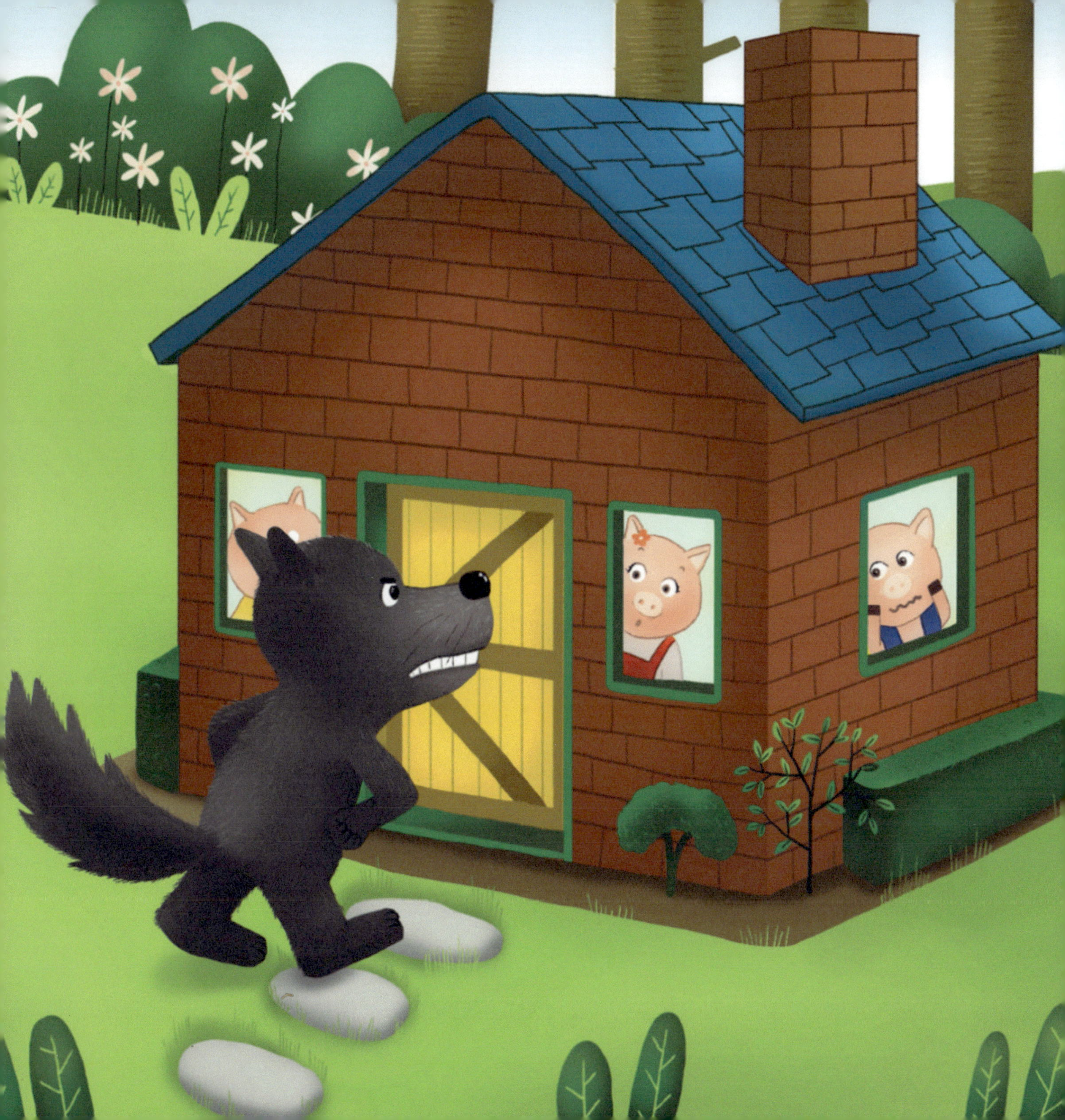

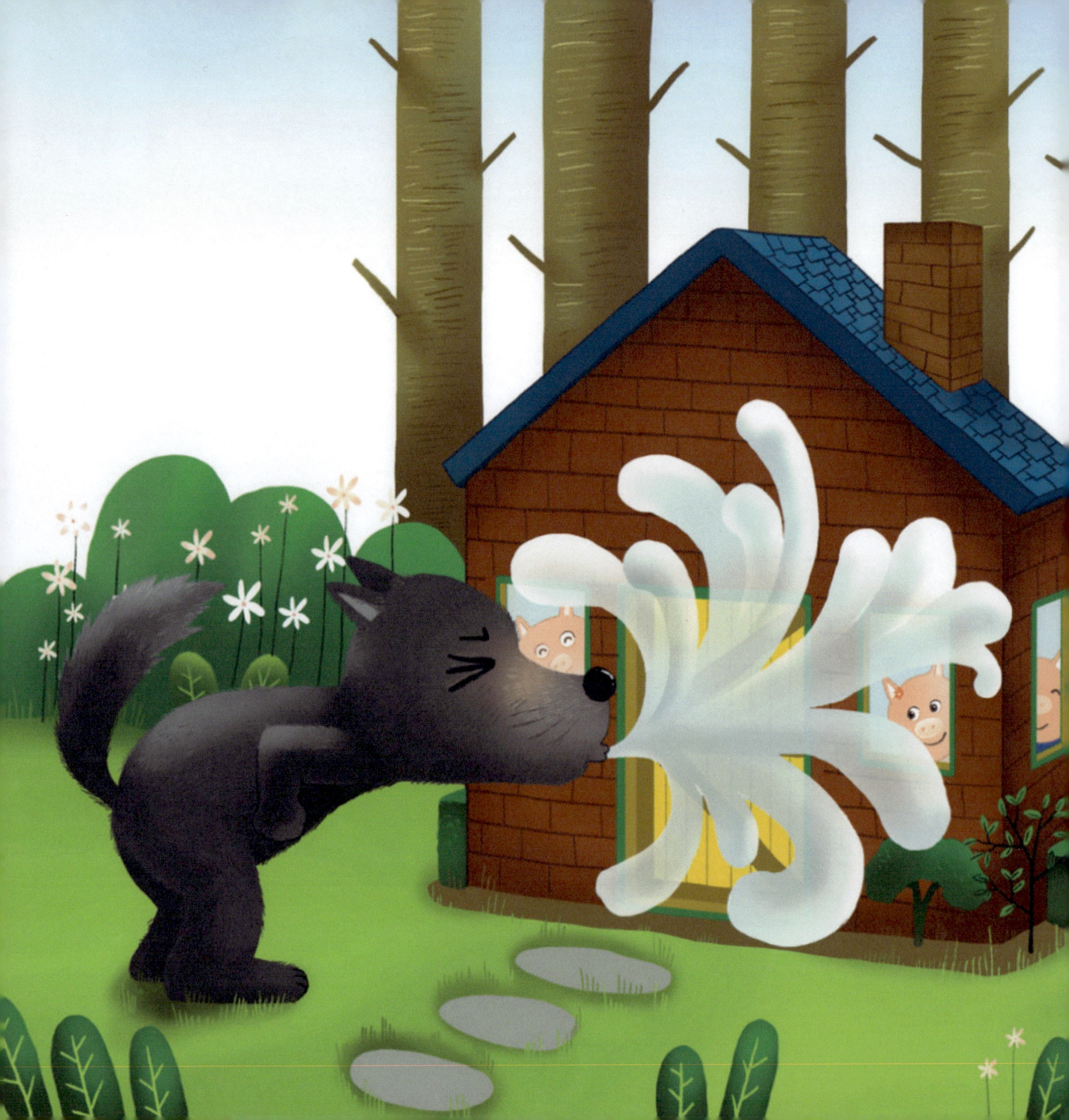

But nothing happened! He blew again!

Mais rien ne se passa ! Il souffla encore !

Still, nothing happened!

Et toujours rien !

"I'll get you! Just you wait!" said the wolf as he went back home.

« Je vais t'avoir ! Attends un peu ! » dit le loup en retournant chez lui.

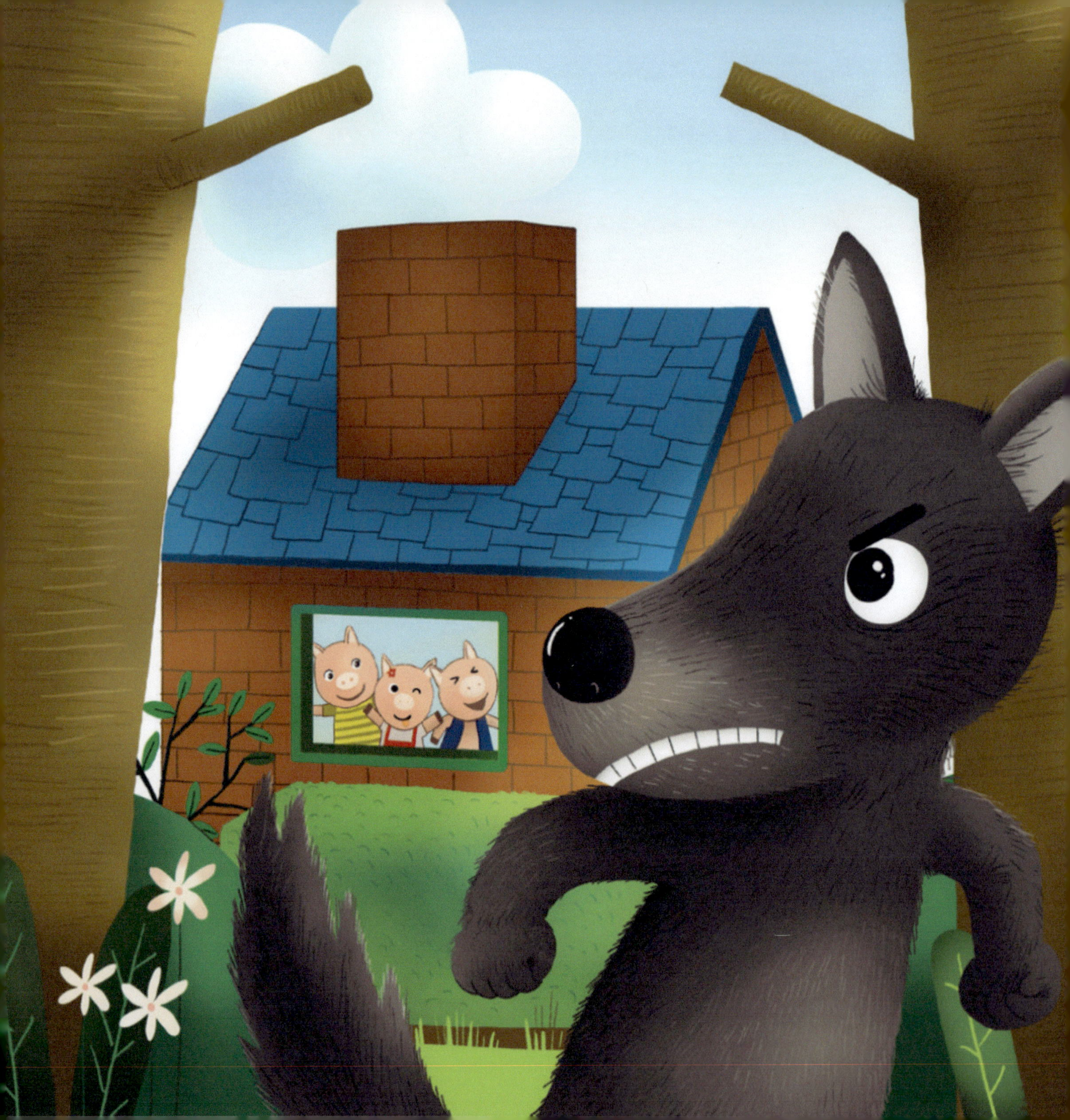

The eldest pig spotted the wolf and knew what he was planning to do.

L'aîné des cochons vit le loup monter sur le toit et comprit ce qu'il voulait faire.

"The wolf is going to come through the chimney!

« Le loup va passer par la cheminée !

Grab the big pot and boil some water! Hurry!"

Prends la grande marmite et fais bouillir de l'eau ! Vite ! »

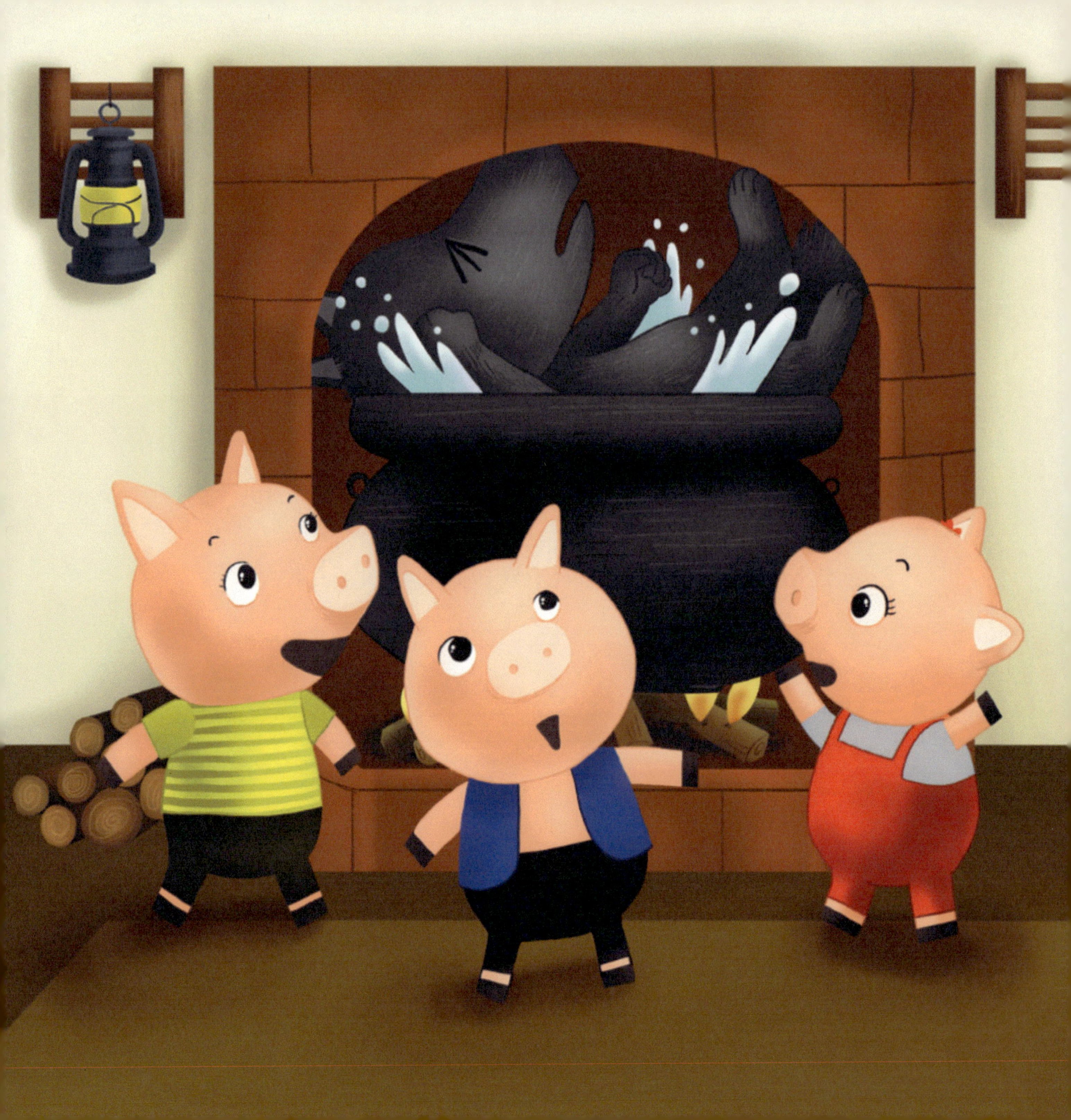

Shortly after, the wolf fell through the chimney and landed in the pot.

Peu de temps après, le loup passa par la cheminée et atterrit dans la marmite.

The wolf was gone!

Le loup avait disparu !

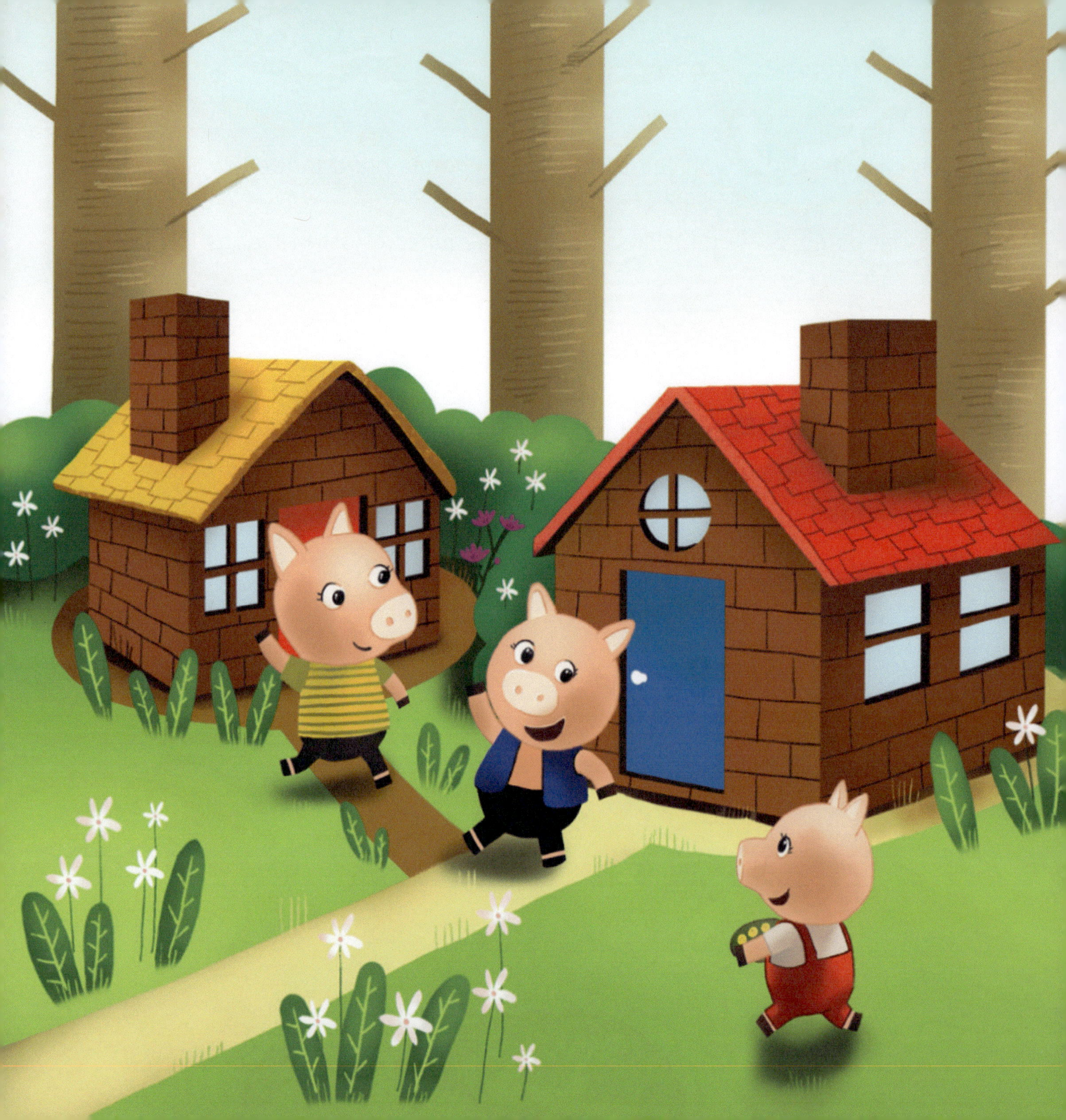

The wolf ran away, never to return!

Le loup s'enfuit, pour ne jamais revenir !

The three little pigs cheered!

Les trois petits cochons se réjouirent !

They rebuilt their houses out of bricks and lived happily ever after.

Ils reconstruisirent leur maison en briques et vécurent heureux pour toujours.

Spot the difference
Trouve la différence

There are 5 to find

Il y a 5 à trouver

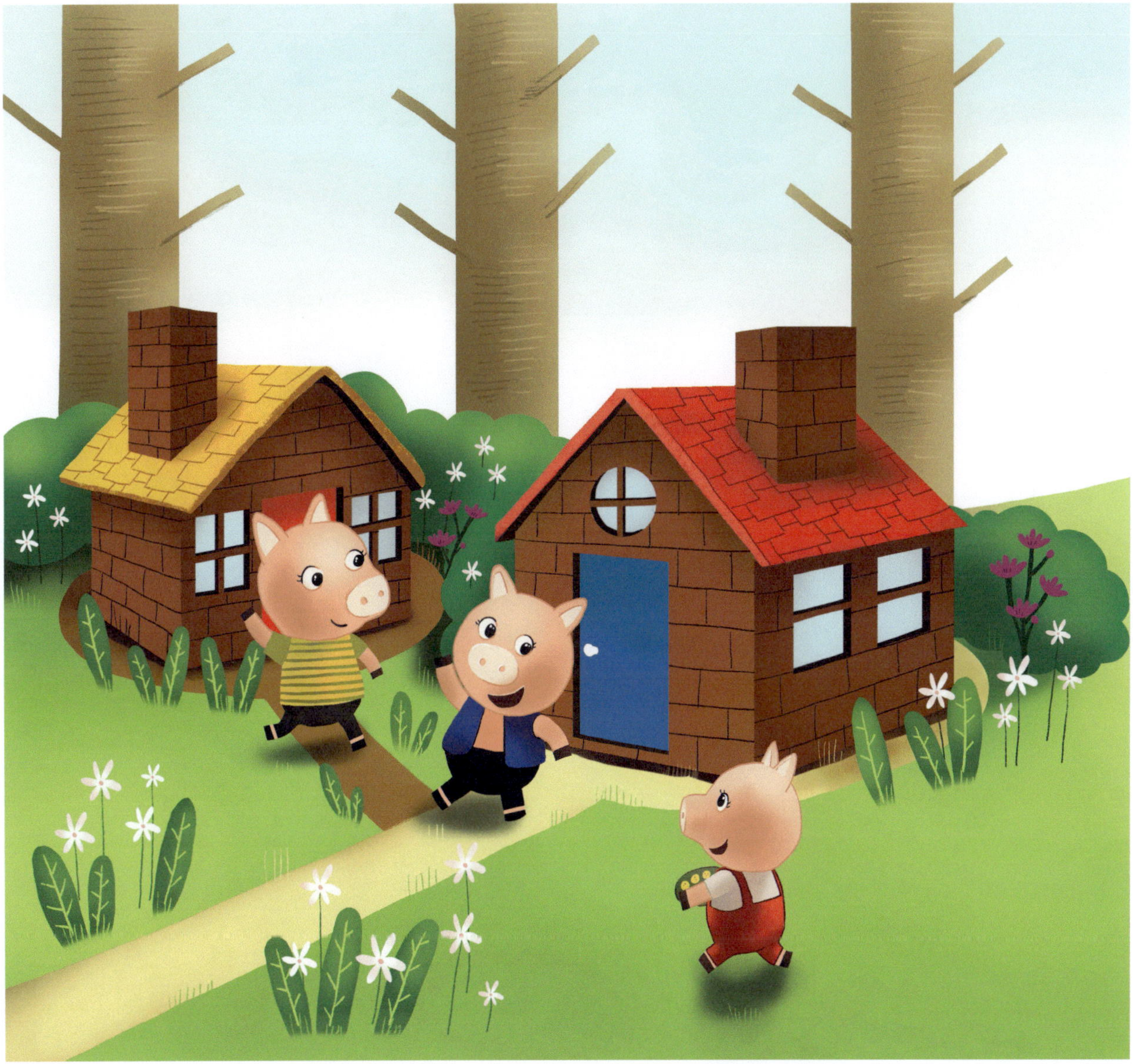

Help the big bad wolf get home!

Aidez le grand méchant loup à rentrer chez lui !

Answers

Réponses

Vocabulary
Vocabulaire

Blue	Bleu	Straw	Paille
Brick	Brique	Wolf	Loup
House	Maison	Wood	Bois
Pig	Cochon	Yellow	Jaune
Red	Rouge		

Other bilingual books

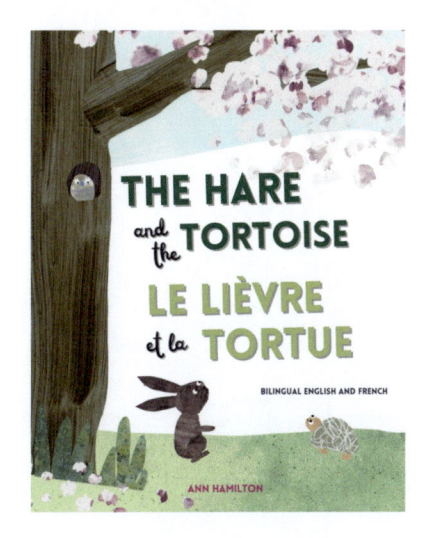

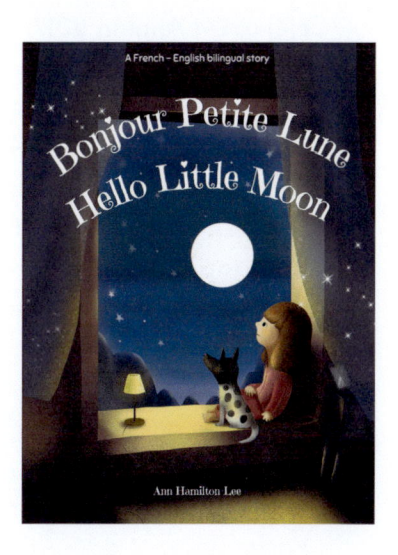

MOOLIPRINT
BILINGUAL BOOKS

Continue your family's bilingual journey by unlocking a fantastic **10% discount** on your next order with the exclusive code COCHONS10 when you shop directly at www.mooliprint.com. *

But there's more to this adventure!
With every purchase you make on our website, we join forces to plant a magnificent new tree, helping to foster a greener tomorrow!

Start saving while making a positive impact on the planet today!

BUY DIRECT!

1 tree planted
with every order

MOOLIPRINT

*Please note that the discount code COCHONS10 can only be redeemed once.

Ann Hamilton-Lee

Hello, I'm Ann! In 2017, I wrote my first book, "Hello Little Moon," inspired by my daughter and our dog. My mission was to create a story that featured them and also showcased a more diverse range of Asian characters in the books we read. Realizing the lack of Chinese language learning materials for families, I decided to write bilingual Chinese books to bridge that gap. Since then, I've received many requests from parents to translate my books into different languages, leading me on an exciting journey.

When I'm not chasing after my family and Monty, our beloved dog, I find solace in writing. My happy place is accompanied by a cup of tea and an egg custard tart, be it Chinese, English or Portuguese - I adore them all!

Free French audio book!

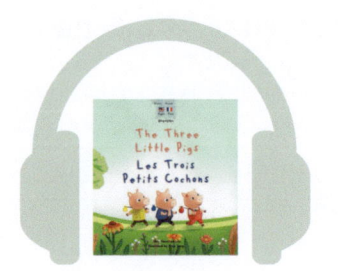

Unlock the captivating audio version of "Les Trois Petite Cochons" by signing up for my newsletter. Be the first to hear about new releases and enjoy exclusive discounts!
visit https://dl.bookfunnel.com/b104wa5h9m or scan the QR code

MOOLI PRINT
BILINGUAL BOOKS

We'd love to hear from you! Leaving a review helps us to create more books!

Printed in France by Amazon
Brétigny-sur-Orge, FR